BLAZERS

SHARK ZONE

MEGAMOUTH SHARK

by Deborah Nuzzolo

Reading Consultant:
Barbara J. Fox
Reading Specialist
North Carolina State University

Content Consultant:
Jody Rake, member
Southwest Marine/Aquatic Educators' Association

CAPSTONE PRESS
a capstone imprint

Blazers is published by Capstone Press,
151 Good Counsel Drive, P.O. Box 669, Mankato, Minnesota 56002.
www.capstonepub.com

Books published by Capstone Press are manufactured with paper
containing at least 10 percent post-consumer waste.

Library of Congress Cataloging-in-Publication Data
Nuzzolo, Deborah.
  Megamouth shark / by Deborah Nuzzolo.
      p. cm—(Blazers. Shark zone)
  Summary: "Describes megamouth sharks, their physical features, and their role in the
ecosystem"—Provided by publisher.
  Includes bibliographical references and index.
  ISBN 978-1-4296-5417-3 (library binding)
  1. Megamouth shark—Juvenile literature. I. Title. II. Series.

  QL638.95.M44N893 2011
  597.3—dc22   2010024773

Editorial Credits
Christopher L. Harbo, editor; Juliette Peters, designer; Eric Manske, production specialist

Photo Credits
© SeaPics.com/Bruce Rasner, 6–7, 9, 10–11, 12, 16, 18–19, 21, 23, 25, 26–27, 28–29;
    Tom Haight, cover, 5, 14–15

Artistic Effects
Shutterstock/artida; Eky Studio; Giuseppe_R

Printed in the United States of America in Stevens Point, Wisconsin.
092010   005934WZS11

TABLE OF CONTENTS

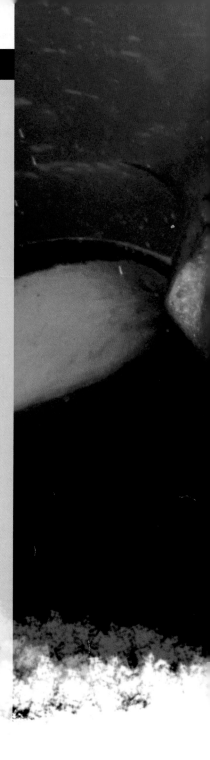

CHAPTER 1

GIANT YAWNERS

A shark rises from the ocean depths. It turns toward a group of plankton. A silver strip in its large, yawning mouth twinkles in the dark sea.

plankton—tiny plants and animals that drift in the sea

yawning—wide open

The megamouth shark's scientific name means "giant yawner of the sea."

The shark glides through the group of plankton. It traps food inside its big mouth. The megamouth shark gulps down its dinner.

CHAPTER 2

OPEN WIDE

Megamouth sharks have large bodies to go along with their big mouths. These huge sharks grow up to 17 feet (5.2 meters) long. They weigh about 1,760 pounds (800 kilograms).

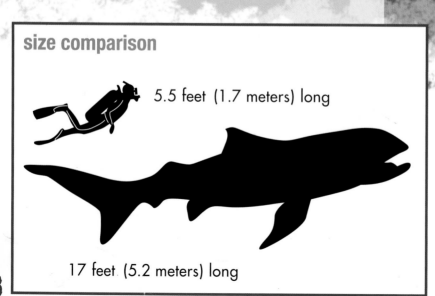

size comparison

5.5 feet (1.7 meters) long

17 feet (5.2 meters) long

SHARK FACT

The largest megamouth shark
ever caught was 23 feet (7 m) long.

The megamouth shark has a short, round **snout**. Its head is long and wide. The head is almost as long as the rest of the body.

snout—the front part of a shark's head that includes the nose, mouth, and jaws

pectoral fins

A megamouth's body is soft and floppy. Its **pectoral fins** are long and narrow. These features make the megamouth a sluggish swimmer.

SHARK FACT

Megamouth sharks have dark backs to help them hide in the deep sea.

pectoral fin—the hard, flat limb on either side of a shark

Megamouth sharks have giant mouths. A silvery strip lines the inside of their mouths. Scientists believe this shiny band may attract prey.

prey—an animal that is hunted by another animal for food

SHARK FACT

Megamouths have more than
50 rows of small, hooked teeth.

For such a large shark, megamouths eat surprisingly small prey. They eat mostly shrimp. They also eat plankton and jellyfish.

SHARK FACT

Megamouth sharks dine at night. They swim near the ocean's surface in search of prey.

Megamouth sharks are filter feeders. To eat, a megamouth sticks out its jaws, sucks in prey, and shuts its mouth. Water exits through the gills. Prey stays in the mouth.

gills

gill—a body part that a fish uses to breathe; gills are the slits on the sides of a shark's head

CHAPTER 3

SWIMMING IN THE SEA

Megamouth sharks live in the Atlantic, Indian, and Pacific oceans. They like warm water. They swim in both shallow and deep water.

Megamouth Sightings

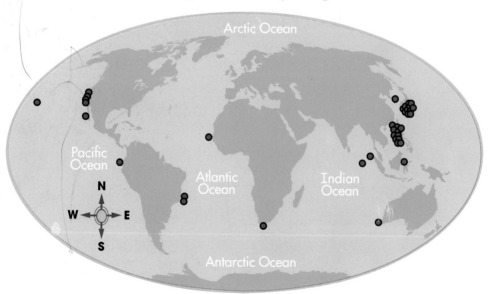

Arctic Ocean

Pacific Ocean

N
W E
S

Atlantic Ocean

Indian Ocean

Antarctic Ocean

● megamouth shark sightings

During the day, megamouths dive deep. They may swim more than 3,200 feet (975 m) below the sea surface.

Megamouth sharks are part of the balance of **predators** and prey in the ocean. They don't compete for food with other large sharks. They live on shrimp and plankton that most other sharks don't eat.

predator—an animal that hunts other animals for food

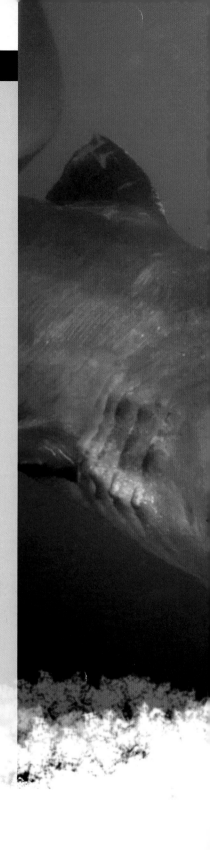

CHAPTER 4

PEACEFUL GIANT

Megamouths are big, but they do not harm people. They have small teeth and eat small food. Swimmers rarely see megamouths because these sharks only swim near the surface at night.

People do not hunt megamouth sharks. But some megamouth sharks have been accidentally caught in fish traps and nets.

SHARK FACT

The megamouth shark was first discovered off the coast of Hawaii in 1976.

Megamouth sharks are mysterious. Less than 50 megamouth sharks have been seen worldwide. Scientists have much more to learn about these amazing sharks.

SHARK FACT

In 1990 scientists tracked a megamouth's movements for two days. They learned that the shark swam in deep water during the day. It swam in shallower water at night.

Glossary

gill (GIL)—a body part that a fish uses to breathe; gills are the slits on the sides of a shark's head

mysterious (miss-TIHR-ee-uhss)—very hard to explain or understand

pectoral fin (PEK-tor-uhl FIN)—the hard, flat limb on either side of a shark

plankton (PLANGK-tuhn)—tiny plants and animals that drift in the sea

predator (PRED-uh-tur)—an animal that hunts other animals for food

prey (PRAY)—an animal hunted by another animal for food

snout (SNOUT)—the front part of a shark's head that includes the nose, mouth, and jaws

yawning (YAWN-ing)—wide open

Read More

Doubilet, David, and Jennifer Hayes. *Face to Face with Sharks.* Washington D.C.: National Geographic, 2009.

MacQuitty, Miranda. *Shark.* DK Eyewitness Books. New York: DK Pub., 2008.

Nuzzolo, Deborah. *Megamouth Shark.* Sharks. Mankato, Minnesota: Capstone Press, 2009.

Internet Sites

FactHound offers a safe, fun way to find Internet sites related to this book. All of the sites on FactHound have been researched by our staff.

Here's all you do:

Visit *www.facthound.com*

Type in this code: 9781429654173

Check out projects, games and lots more at
www.capstonekids.com

Index